What Can We Do About ACID RAIN?

David J. Jakubiak

PowerKiDS press.

New York

For Ted Williams, who taught me about the brook trout

Published in 2012 by The Rosen Publishing Group, Inc.
29 East 21st Street, New York, NY 10010

First Edition

Editor: Amelie von Zumbusch
Book Design: Kate Laczynski
Layout Design: Julio Gil

Photo Credits: Cover Richard Packwood/Photolibrary/Getty Images; p. 4 Lori Adamski Peek/Workbook Stock/Getty Images; pp. 6, 18 Shutterstock.com; p. 8 Mitchell Funk/Getty Images; p. 10 Picavet/Botanica/Getty Images; p. 12 Oliver Strewe/Stone/Getty Images; p. 14 Panoramic Images/Getty Images; p. 16 Ed Darack/Science Faction/Getty Images; p. 20 Eco Images/Universal Images Group/Getty Images.

Library of Congress Cataloging-in-Publication Data

Jakubiak, David J.
  What can we do about acid rain? / by David J. Jakubiak. — 1st ed.
      p. cm. — (Protecting our planet)
  Includes bibliographical references and index.
  ISBN 978-1-4488-4984-0 (library binding) — ISBN 978-1-4488-5116-4 (pbk.) —
  ISBN 978-1-4488-5117-1 (6-pack)
  1. Acid rain—Juvenile literature. I. Title.
  TD195.44.J35 2012
  363.738'66—dc22
                                                        2010053329

Manufactured in the United States of America

CPSIA Compliance Information: Batch #WS11PK: For Further Information contact Rosen Publishing, New York, New York at 1-800-237-9932

CONTENTS

There are many kinds of acids. You have an acid called gastric acid in your stomach. It breaks down the food you eat.

Something in the Smoke

Smoke enters the air every day. It streams from cars and trucks. It drifts out of the chimneys on houses. It pumps from the **smokestacks** of factories and power plants. Smoke is mostly **water vapor**, or water in the form of gas. However, there are also other gases in smoke. When some of these gases mix with water vapor in the air, acid rain forms. This acid rain falls to Earth. There, the rain hurts plants and animals.

Acids, such as acid rain, cause changes in other kinds of matter. Strong acids can burn or eat away at other matter. One kind of acid makes lemon juice bitter. Another acid makes vinegar sour.

Plants and animals depend on rain for the water they need to live. When rain becomes acid rain, though, it hurts these living things.

When the Sun beats down on Earth, it warms seas, lakes, and other water. This makes some of the water turn into water vapor. As gases do, the vapor rises into the **atmosphere**. The atmosphere is the layers of air around Earth. In the atmosphere, vapor sometimes cools down. This makes it turn back into liquid water. The drops of liquid water form clouds. Sometimes, they fall to Earth as rain.

When certain gases mix with the water vapor in the atmosphere, the rain that forms is acidic. Acid snow can form, too. This happens when droplets of acid rain in the atmosphere freeze into snowflakes.

DID YOU KNOW?

Fog forms when water vapor cools and forms a cloud near the ground. If gases have made this water vapor acidic, acid fog can form.

Cars, vans, buses, and trucks all produce the gases that cause acid rain. When it falls, acid rain eats away at the paint on these things.

The gases that cause acid rain get into the atmosphere in several ways. One natural cause is **volcanoes**. Volcanoes are places where melted rock and gases from inside Earth break through the ground. Some of the gases that escape from volcanoes can cause acid rain.

Gases that cause acid rain also enter the atmosphere as a result of things people do. These gases form when people burn **fossil fuels**, such as coal and oil. People burn fossil fuels in power plants to make **electricity**. Many things, from computers to night-lights to refrigerators, run on electricity. People also use oil to make **gasoline**. Most cars, trucks, and buses run on gasoline.

This fish is a trout. Trout can deal with higher acid levels than bass can. Perch can put up with water that is even more acidic, though.

Lakes, ponds, streams, rivers, and wetlands are full of plants and animals that need fresh, clean water. When acid rain falls or flows into a lake or other body of water, that body of water can become acidic. Small changes in how acidic the water is can mean big trouble for things living there. Fish, frog, and salamander eggs will not hatch if the water they are laid in is too acidic. Too much acid kills adult fish, too.

Different animals and plants can stand different levels of acid in water. Shellfish, such as snails, cannot put up with much acid at all. Even if an animal can stand a fair amount of acid, acid rain can cause problems. It may kill off the plants or animals that that animal eats.

This forest of fir trees in the Czech Republic has been hurt by acid rain. Acid rain has hurt a lot of forests in central Europe.

Streams, ponds, and lakes are not the only places hurt by acid rain. It causes problems in forests, too. Acid rain slows down the growth of trees. It makes leaves and pine needles turn brown. It hurts roots.

Acid rain sinks deep into the soil. This causes problems for trees. Acid rain uncovers metals that are bad for plants. It also washes away **nutrients** in the soil. These are things that trees need to grow. Acid rain causes the most problems in places with thin soil. These places are often forests in the mountains. For example, the Appalachian Mountains in the northeastern United States are troubled by acid rain.

DID YOU KNOW?

Acid clouds and fog surround some mountaintop forests. This is another reason that acid rain causes so many problems there.

Acid rain has eaten away at these gravestones. Older gravestones are more likely to be harmed by acid rain because they were made of softer stones.

Washed Away

Plants and animals suffer when acid rain falls on forests or bodies of water. Cities and towns can be hurt by acid rain as well. Over time, acid rain can eat away at buildings made of stone and brick. Acid rain is especially a problem for things made from certain stones, such as limestone and marble. The paint on cars and trucks can be worn away by acid rain, too.

The effects of acid rain are often seen on statues and gravestones. The words on some of the oldest gravestones in the United States have been slowly erased by acid rain. The faces of gargoyles on many old buildings have been wiped away, too.

16

These smokestacks are part of New Mexico's Cholla Power Plant. This coal-burning plant put in scrubbers in the 2000s.

Though people have caused most acid rain, we have also taken steps to end it. In 1990, the United States started the Acid Rain Program to slow down acid rain. The program set limits on how much of certain gases factories and power plants could put out. Many factories and power plants put **scrubbers** on their smokestacks. These tools clean the smoke. The scrubbers cost a lot of money but work well.

In 2010, a report from the U.S. government showed that the amount of **sulfur dioxide** being produced had dropped. Sulfur dioxide is one of the gases that makes acid rain. In 1980, 17.3 tons (15.7 t) of sulfur dioxide was pumped into the sky. In 2009, just 5.7 tons (5.2 t) was produced.

These turbines are part of a wind farm. Texas, Iowa, and California are among the U.S. states with the most wind farms.

Another way to put an end to acid rain would be to stop burning fossil fuels in power plants. Today people are turning to new ways of making electricity. For example, **solar panels** take in energy from the sun. This energy can be used to warm houses, heat water, or make electricity. **Wind turbines** capture the wind's energy to make electricity. They look a bit like huge pinwheels. **Wind farms** are made up of lots of turbines. They can produce lots of electricity.

If people used cars less, it would cut down on the gases that produce acid rain. There is also a push to make cars and trucks that do not run on gasoline.

DID YOU KNOW?

California is one of the leaders in clean energy. A state law there says that by 2020, one-third of the state's power must come from clean energy.

Here, people are dropping lime into a lake that was made acidic by acid rain. Lime helps cancel out acid, so people use it to treat acidic lakes.

In the 1980s, acid rain was a big problem. Trees in many parts of the eastern United States and Canada were dying. Scientists and fishermen were finding lakes without fish. The rain was destroying statues. Today, things have gotten a lot better. Laws that limit the release of gases that cause acid rain seem to be working. Some lakes that were troubled by acid rain once again have plants, fish, and other animals living in them.

Other things hurt by acid rain have been slower to heal. When nutrients wash out of soil, it takes a long time for them to come back. Once the writing on gravestones is eaten away by acid rain, it is gone forever.

Stand Up for Clean Rain

Producing electricity is one of the main causes of acid rain. Using less electricity helps cut down on acid rain. Remember to turn out the lights when you leave a room. Do not leave the TV on if you are not watching it. Wear warm clothes in the winter instead of turning the heat up high.

Acid rain is not as much of a problem in the United States today as it was in the 1980s. This shows that people really can help turn environmental problems around. It is important that we continue to move forward, though. We must keep moving toward cleaner energy. This will lead to cleaner rain.

GLOSSARY

atmosphere (AT-muh-sfeer) The gases around an object in space. On Earth this is air.

electricity (ih-lek-TRIH-suh-tee) Power that produces light, heat, or movement.

fossil fuels (FO-sul FYOOLZ) Fuels, such as coal, natural gas, or gasoline, that were made from plants that died millions of years ago.

gasoline (GA-suh-leen) A liquid made from oil. Cars run on gasoline.

nutrients (NOO-tree-ents) Food that a living thing needs to live and grow.

scrubbers (SKRUH-berz) Things put on smokestacks to clean the smoke.

smokestacks (SMOHK-staks) Tall towers that let smoke out of factories and power plants.

solar panels (SOH-ler PA-nulz) Objects that take in and store solar energy.

sulfur dioxide (SUL-fur dy-OK-syd) A gas that causes acid rain.

volcanoes (vol-KAY-nohz) Openings that sometimes shoots up hot, melted rock called lava.

water vapor (WAH-ter VAY-pur) The gaseous state of water.

wind farms (WIND FAHRMZ) Places where lots of wind turbines are set up to make electricity.

wind turbines (WIND TUR-bunz) Machines that make power using the wind's movement.

INDEX

WEB SITES

Due to the changing nature of Internet links, PowerKids Press has developed an online list of Web sites related to the subject of this book. This site is updated regularly. Please use this link to access the list:
www.powerkidslinks.com/pop/acidrain/